Little People, BIG DREAMS
SIMONE DE BEAUVOIR

Written by
Mª Isabel Sánchez Vegara

Illustrated by
Christine Roussey

Lincoln
Children's Books

Simone Lucie Ernestine Marie was born into a wealthy family in France. She lived in an elegant house in the city of Paris, with her parents, little sister, and servants.

From an early age, Simone's father encouraged her to read and write. He often told her that she had the brain of a man... "But why is a boy's mind different than a girl's?" Simone thought.

Overnight, her family lost their fortune. Her mother took on the housework, while her father did little to help. Simone thought this was unfair. She had become a feminist before the word even existed!

Her parents managed to save enough money to send Simone
and her sister to a prestigious Catholic school.

Her father sent them to study so they could earn a living by themselves—without relying on a man for money.

But when Simone turned 14, she started
to question everything she had ever learned.
Some questions were really tricky to answer, like
"Does God exist?" She wasn't so sure anymore...

Simone decided to go to college and become a philosopher:
that's someone who loves finding new ways of thinking.
But she wanted to become a writer, too. So, she began
a journal and started to write her first stories.

One day, she joined a group
of students all preparing for the
same exam—and met a young
man named Jean-Paul Sartre.

He was not just her
soul mate, he was
her mind mate, too!

Simone and Jean-Paul never married or lived under the same roof, but they lived their love story in their own unique way.

After college, Simone became a teacher.
She was teaching in Paris when World War II
broke out. She spent a lot of time alone and wrote
more than ever. Soon, her first novel was published.

It caused a scandal when it first came out—
readers were shocked. Simone was the
first person to write about women
making their own choices.

Over the following years, Simone had many adventures. She wrote books and met other revolutionaries trying to change the world, just like her.

Simone kept writing for the rest of her life,
inspiring women around the world.
They called her the "mother of feminism."

And thanks to little Simone, we now know that we're not born men or women—just special human beings with a life full of choices to make.

SIMONE DE BEAUVOIR

(Born 1908 • Died 1986)

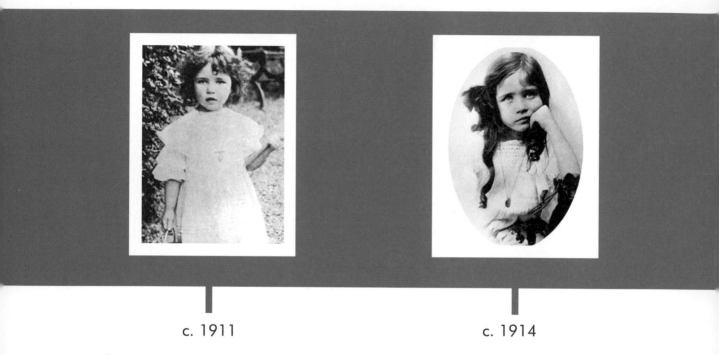

c. 1911   c. 1914

Simone de Beauvoir was born in Paris, France, to a wealthy family.
Shortly after World War I, her family lost most of their fortune. In
spite of this, her parents still sent Simone to a private school. They
knew she would have to be well educated in order to earn a living by
herself, without relying on a husband. Young women were expected
to get married at that time, and her family didn't have enough money
for a dowry (an amount of riches that was passed from the bride's
family to her husband when they married). So, Simone used her
freedom from marriage to study subjects that interested her. She went
to college and gained a degree in philosophy, and then a higher
degree on top of that. At 21, she became the youngest person to
pass one of the most prestigious philosophy exams in France. While

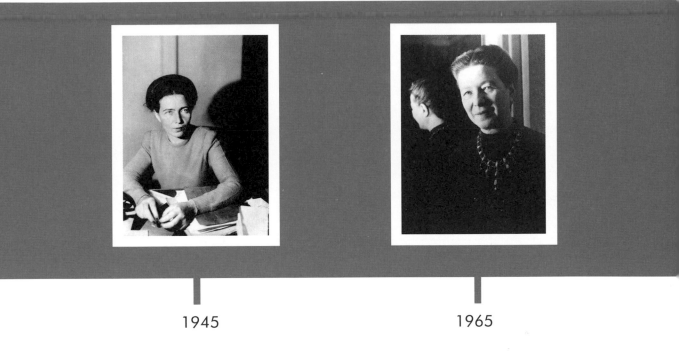

1945

1965

studying, she met Jean-Paul Sartre, a like-minded thinker and the man who would become her life partner. Together, they shared ideas and supported each other—but they never married. Simone went on to write many texts, both fiction and nonfiction. She said in her most famous book, that "one is not born, but rather becomes, a woman." Simone showed that as we grow up, we learn behaviors and ways of thinking that can create inequality between men and women. The book was revolutionary, as it introduced the idea that we all have choices to make about how we live our lives. Simone lived her life courageously, putting into practice ideas that formed foundations for the women's movement decades later. And she was full of hope for change in the future, saying "the free woman is just being born."

Want to find out more about **Simone de Beauvoir?**
Read one of these great books:

Philosophy for Kids by David White
Children's Book of Philosophy by DK

If you're in Paris, France, you could visit the famous Café de Flore, where
Simone used to write her revolutionary works.

Brimming with creative inspiration, how-to projects, and useful
information to enrich your everyday life, Quarto Knows is a favorite
destination for those pursuing their interests and passions. Visit our
site and dig deeper with our books into your area of interest:
Quarto Creates, Quarto Cooks, Quarto Homes, Quarto Lives,
Quarto Drives, Quarto Explores, Quarto Gifts, or Quarto Kids.

Text © 2018 Mª Isabel Sánchez Vegara. Illustrations © 2018 Christine Roussey

First Published in the U.S.A in 2018 by Lincoln Children's Books, an imprint of The Quarto Group.

400 First Avenue North, Suite 400, Minneapolis, MN 55401, USA.

T (612) 344-8100 F (612) 344-8692 **www.QuartoKnows.com**

First Published in Spain in 2018 under the title Pequeña & Grande Simone de Beauvoir

by Alba Editorial, s.l.u., Baixada de Sant Miquel, 1, 08002 Barcelona

www.albaeditorial.es

All rights reserved.

Published by arrangement with Alba Editorial, s.l.u. Translation rights arranged by IMC Agència Literària, SL

All rights reserved.

ISBN 978-1-78603-232-4

The illustrations were created with pencil, colored pencils, and digital techniques. Set in Futura BT.

Published by Rachel Williams • Designed by Karissa Santos

Edited by Katy Flint • Production by Jenny Cundill

Manufactured in Guangdong, China CC092018

9 7 5 3 1 2 4 6 8

Photographic acknowledgements (pages 28–29, from left to right) 1. Simone de Beauvoir, child c. 1911 © Tallandier / Bridgeman Images 2.
Simone de Beauvoir (1908–1986), child c.1914 © Tallandier / Bridgeman Images 3. Simone de Beauvoir (1908–1986), 1945 © / Private
Collection / Roger-Viollet, Paris / Bridgeman Images 4. Simone de Beauvoir, 1965 © CSU Archives/Everett Collection / Bridgeman Images

Collect the *Little People,* **BIG DREAMS** series:

FRIDA KAHLO

ISBN: 978-1-84780-783-0

COCO CHANEL

ISBN: 978-1-84780-784-7

MAYA ANGELOU
ISBN: 978-1-84780-889-9

AMELIA EARHART
ISBN: 978-1-84780-888-2

AGATHA CHRISTIE

ISBN: 978-1-84780-960-5

MARIE CURIE

ISBN: 978-1-84780-962-9

ROSA PARKS
ISBN: 978-1-78603-018-4

AUDREY HEPBURN

ISBN: 978-1-78603-053-5

EMMELINE PANKHURST

ISBN: 978-1-78603-020-7

ELLA FITZGERALD

ISBN: 978-1-78603-087-0

ADA LOVELACE

ISBN: 978-1-78603-076-4

JANE AUSTEN

ISBN: 978-1-78603-120-4

GEORGIA O'KEEFFE

ISBN: 978-1-78603-122-8

HARRIET TUBMAN

ISBN: 978-1-78603-227-0

ANNE FRANK

ISBN: 978-1-78603-229-4

MOTHER TERESA

ISBN: 978-1-78603-230-0

JOSEPHINE BAKER

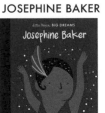
ISBN: 978-1-78603-228-7

L. M. MONTGOMERY

ISBN: 978-1-78603-233-1

JANE GOODALL
ISBN: 978-1-78603-231-7

SIMONE DE BEAUVOIR
ISBN: 978-1-78603-232-4

Now in board book format:

COCO CHANEL

ISBN: 978-1-78603-245-4

MAYA ANGELOU
ISBN: 978-1-78603-249-2

FRIDA KAHLO
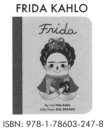
ISBN: 978-1-78603-247-8

AMELIA EARHART

ISBN: 978-1-78603-251-5

MARIE CURIE

ISBN: 978-1-78603-253-9